MW00941198

# MANIPULATION

Proven Manipulation Techniques
To Influence People with NLP,
Mind Control And Persuasion!

Pete Martin & Nataly Myers

© 2016 Copyright.

Text copyright reserved by Pete Martin & Nataly Myers

The contents of this book may not be reproduced, duplicated or transmitted without direct written permission from the authors

Disclaimer : all attempts have been made by the author to provide factual and accurate content. No responsibility will be taken by the authors for any damages caused by misuse of the content described in this book. The content of this book has been derived from various sources. Please consult a licensed professional before attempting any techniques outlined in this book.

# Table of Contents

**Chapter 11: Scientifically Proven Methods of Non-Verbal Influence**

**Chapter 12: The Social Psychology of Making Friends**

**Conclusion**

# Introduction

Social psychology is a complex discipline that refers to the interplay of human emotions, perceptions and behaviors arising from the influences inherent in culture and environment. We all have our way of looking at the world. What social psychology hopes to achieve is to explain why certain people look at the world in one way and others, differently. While we're all human (and subject to all the slings and arrows to which that flesh is heir), we are all unique.

Without even knowing it, we are influenced by everything around us. The good, the bad and the ugly all contribute to who we are socially; how we interact with and perceive others. Sometimes these influences can skew our perceptions to an enormous degree. The influence of media (especially the new, 24/7 variety) and television, particularly, create an environment in which our emotions, behaviors and perceptions are formed.

Essentially, this discipline forms a bridge between sociology and psychology, with the two areas informing each other toward a more fulsome understanding of what makes people do and say the things they do when interacting with others. This discipline addresses not only individual response, but also responses seen in groups of people and has led to the term "group dynamics". This term expresses the hierarchical nature of people when forming groups of any kind. Someone is always dominant in group situations. Leaders emerge.

Followers fall in line. This is the common architecture of human relationships, no matter how large or small, or whether they're casually organized or institutional. Family and social groups and workplace associations and factions – all these human groupings are subject to group dynamics and their inevitable impact on the quality of the relationships involved.

This is the basis of social psychology. Most people are at least marginally aware of it, while perhaps not grasping its fundamental importance in the conduct of human affairs. This discipline forms the foundation of this book, because perception, emotion and behavior, when keenly observed, can be influenced and directed through the subtle employment of a variety of methods that I'll describe to you, so you can use them. In essence, this book represents a popular interpretation of a discipline that renders it more accessible. The aspects of social psychology discussed in this book concern applications that can be applied more broadly, toward an enhanced understanding of the people we meet every day. This forms a broader discipline than that described above. I'm going to detail for you a variety of communication tricks that can help you develop your career swiftly and effectively. There are also the techniques discussed here that can influence people toward the advancement of your goals, as well as those held in common in workplaces. By learning to understand the dynamics that are in play in all our social interactions, we can gain a better command of our function in the world and more effectively manoeuver our ways through it.

As you will appreciate while reading this book, people react more to non-verbal communication than they do to speeches and conversations. In fact, it's known that 75% of all communication is non-verbal. So it is only reasonable that you should pay close attention to how you come across to others in terms of your body language, mannerisms and facial expressions. Even the way you hold yourself and the way you dress is information that is read by others. The same is true of everyone. When you're aware of these non-verbal sources of information, you can read and take advantage of them. It is important that you learn the tips provided in this book about how to read various physical signals. As explained herein, some of these signals are so subtle that an untrained eye might think little of them. Yet, the ability to read these signals can result in a greater mastery of social situations and business situations that can make you a leader in your social circle, or workplace.

In this book, you will not just learn how to communicate effectively without speaking, you will also learn how to influence people by transmitting appropriate and compelling body language. You'll learn to read what people are withholding, as signaled to you by their body language. There is important information in every eye movement, every hand gesture, body position, stance and facial expression. All this information can be read, if you're aware and have learned to decipher the silent language employed by the human body in social discourse. Subtext is not just for words. It's also spoken by the actions of the body, the pitch of the voice, its tone and word selection. It's written in our intonations and our sartorial choices. In fact, we are walking, open books which can be read by those who are well-versed in the study of non-verbal communication and its role in social interactions.


In short, this book teaches you some simple methods of getting things done the way you want them done, by influencing those around you with the information they freely offer via their body language mannerisms and other non-verbal cues. It will also teach you how to use your own body language to break down communicative barriers and establish the kind of rapport you need, to build consensus with others. You will see how efficient you can be in your work and how much more effective you can be in your interactions with others, when you master these psychological and communicative techniques and are able to put them to use. After reading this book, you will have the tools you need to make your communication highly effective and to make your social interactions more successful and fruitful. Happy reading and all the best in your efforts to sharpen and expand your communicative lexicon to encompass those things that transcend words!

# Chapter 1: Why Do People Do the Things They Do?

Everyone reading this will be aware that psychology is concerned with the workings of the mind and how it relates to behavior. When it comes to this disciplinary amalgam called social psychology, you are not just dealing with the way your mind works, you're also incorporating social, environmental and cultural factors, including your interactions with others, whether verbal or non-verbal. Sociology and psychology, following World War II, began to examine the intersection between the two disciplines and how they might inform each other toward a better understanding of why people do the things they do and behave the way they do, in various settings.

The father of social psychology is Norman Triplett. In 1898, he identified the term "social facilitation" to describe the tendency of people to behave differently in public than they do in private. Triplett described three major theoretical streams in identifying this tendency. Activation was the term he used to describe how arousal (response to external stimuli) relates to social interactions and informs them. Evaluation relates to the way people tailor their responses when in the presence of others who will be evaluating them (also called the audience effect). Attention refers to the way in which external stimuli distract us in the course of our social interactions and may impair our ability to engage.

Triplett's theories are the first instance of the disciplines of sociology and psychology being merged in order to arrive at the function of psychology as a feature of social interactions. The three theoretical worlds described by Norman Triplett represent psycho-social lenses through which it's possible to examine the way we engage with each other and how psychological realities drive that engagement.

In our social interactions, we're much more than our inherent mannerisms and idiosyncrasies. We're a world of experiences, cultural presumptions and social constructs. To better understand why people behave the way they do, a good place to start is by examining your own reactions and responsive behaviors in confrontation of the way in which others behave. How do you react to certain situations?

A man is running down the street naked. Do you laugh, or do you scream? Maybe you call the police. Maybe you rip off your clothes and run along with him! Any of these reactions makes perfect sense to the person pursuing them, but which of them is going to seem more normative? That will vary greatly from culture to culture and from person to person. And while our responses to any number of incidents, events, situations and stimuli may be somewhat culturally and socially-mandated, they're also highly individual and also, well within our ability to choose. We're not puppets in a play, controlled by an invisible puppet master who pulls our strings and makes us dance. We choose our responses. We choose our reactions and actions.

While you're going to feel the heat in the kitchen, how you respond to it is a matter of choice. You either mop your brow and carry on, or run for the door, pulling at your clothes; gasping for air. Then again, it is pretty difficult to be sad at the circus! Most people love a good show. Some people, though, fear clowns. Others feel badly for the animals, so while the exception proves the rule, the truth is that our responses are all highly individual.

Your responses are not pre-determined, even though it's pretty easy to predict responses in certain situations (with varying success, as shown above). But if that's so, then you can learn how to tailor your own behavior to present a more unruffled and confident image to others. Ultimately, you are in command of your own responses. By the same token, you are in command of your ability to engage people at a much deeper and more effective level, when you're able to accurately interpret what's going on underneath their words. Remembering that Triplett pointed to the fact that people behave differently in public situations than they do in private ones, we can think of the people around us emotional onions. Just like us, they're full of layers. What the surface tells us can be deceptive, until we begin peeling it back to reveal the next layer and the next, after that.

People have many good reasons for this tendency to conceal the true selves in public. Some of that has to do with trust. Sometimes, they prefer to hide their true natures for fear of not being liked. Other times, they feel it's to their advantage not to show their hand until it's time to play it. For every person on earth, there's a unique set of motivations for the modelling of two faces. This is not necessarily consciously pursued to deceive others. It's more a matter of self-preservation and that's part of the natural, human survival instinct.

# Chapter 2: The Masks We Wear – Emotional Responses

No one is immune to emotional responses. They're human and nobody's perfect. If you think about it seriously, living plants also react to stimuli other than water and sunshine. Haven't you heard about plants responding to the sound of certain types of music positively? The Daily Mail of April 2013, reported that scientific studies had demonstrated that plants reacted differently to heavy metal music than to soft, ambient music. And if you are tempted to take the studies cited with a grain of salt, then let's look at the findings of Dorothy Retallack, who worked with other scientists to establish how playing a variety of music around plants influenced their reactions.

The result of Retallack's experiments, conducted in 1973, are compiled in her book *The Sound of Music and Plants*. Retallack's experiments were carried out at a women's university equipped with soundproof chambers. In each of these, she placed a plant and played a variety of different types of music in each chamber to gauge the reactions of the plants (if any). But what Retallack's experiments revealed is quite astounding.

One of her research's most compelling discoveries is that a continuous monotone killed the plants. Unbroken, 24-hours a day, the sound of the same tone killed the plants rather quickly. However, when tonal variations were played throughout the course of the day, at various times (not continuously), the plants exposed to them flourished.

I think this tells you something about the nature of life. Like plants, human beings are not designed to operate to an emotional monotone. We are creatures of emotional diversity. We like variety and we have different emotions. Exposed to the right stimuli, we can not only survive, but thrive. Those stimuli can come from other people and when they're positive, we tend to thrive. Encouragement, support and co-operative behavior feed us. Conversely, the monotonous banality of sameness can kill us. We need more than water and sunshine, just like plants. We need positive stimuli from the world around us in order to flourish.

Closer to home, you may have seen a plant that goes by the name Touch Me Not. Do you think that is just a whimsical name someone came up with? Far from it – the name means just what it says. Touching this plant causes a reflexive withdrawal of its leaves in response to the stimulus. The plant reacts in the same way you do when somebody pokes a finger in your face, or touches you unexpectedly. You flinch and then, recoil. But when someone touches your arm to underline a point, or pats you on the back, you feel quite differently. Environmental stimuli and their effect on our psychological makeup and the role that plays in our social interactions, form a part of the complex nature of human interplay. There is a lot underneath the human hood and taking it all into consideration is a lot of work. But there are many clues (both verbal and non-verbal) which can provide us with the information we need to more adeptly navigate the world around us.

There's a Swahili saying which describes the role of non-verbal communication rather succinctly: *"Akufukuzaye hakwambii toka"*. This translates as "he who doesn't want you around need not tell you to get out". You know the feeling, I'm sure. You arrive in a room full of people. You're just starting to feel comfortable when you look up and realize that an old enemy is standing nearby, glaring at you. Without saying a word, your common history rears up between you. You can practically cut it with a knife. Others may even sense the silent interchange between you. Personal history has now pierced the veil of the public world and interpolated itself into an otherwise pleasant experience. Either you spend the evening avoiding your nemesis, or you turn tail and flee. Either way, without a word exchanged, the message has been sent that the evening is going to be an uncomfortable one, whether you've chosen it or not.

Is there a way that an incident like the one described above might be managed more effectively? I certainly think so. In fact, I know very well that it can be easily defused. Here's how the foregoing scenario might have played out differently, had you been less willing to bow to the intimidation of a pair of icy eyes trained your way:


You arrive in a room full of people. You're just starting to feel comfortable when you look up and realize that an old enemy is standing nearby, glaring at you. Without saying a word, your common history rears up between you. You can practically cut it with a knife. Others may even sense the silent interchange between you. Personal history has now pierced the veil of the public world and interpolated itself into an otherwise pleasant experience. Either you spend the evening avoiding your nemesis, or you turn tail and flee. Either way, without a word exchanged, the message has been sent that the evening is going to be an uncomfortable one, whether you've chosen it or not. But you choose to push the evening's events in the direction you desire. Holding the gaze of the person glaring at you, you break into a smile and nod your head, then turn away. The gesture may be noticed by others, or not. It doesn't matter. You've responded non-verbally, indicating that you won't be intimidated and further, that you're remaining in the room and enjoying the presence of the other people there. You have acknowledged your old enemy, without having either thrown down a fresh gauntlet or capitulated to a silent demand that you remove yourself from the situation.

# Chapter 3: Non-Verbal Communication

The example in the previous chapter demonstrates one simple way in which non-verbal communication can help you take control of your life and also, influence others. Knowing where you are and who you're with concern more than geography and facial recognition. Understanding the subtext of human interactions is a means of managing them more effectively. Understand the meaning of a glare thrown at you from across a crowded room by someone who doesn't like it is pretty simple. What's not so simple is your decision about formulating a response, right then and there. In understanding what people are trying to tell you without words, you gain a confidence in your social interactions based on wisdom about people. It takes time to learn. It is, in fact, a life's work, but there's much you can do right now to improve your ability to more accurately gauge what people around you are thinking, feeling and perhaps, hoping will happen, where you're concerned.

Here are some common ways people speak without words:

## *Hand gestures*

In some cultures, hand gestures can easily be read by others. In fact, every culture in the world uses them. In some cultures, though, hand gestures have communicative pride of place. One of these is, of course, Italy. In fact, the people of Italy are rather notorious for their tendency to talk with their hands.

Some of these gestures are found in other cultures, but many are peculiar to Italy. Italian art can be seen to feature some of these, like the *ficha* (meaning "fig"), in which the four fingers are brought together with the thumb. Today, this gesture is used to express a capacity crowd in a public facility (restaurant, sports arena, coffee shop). Alternatively, the same gesture when accompanied by a pointed back and forth motion of the upper arm, bent at the elbow means "what?", or "what in the hell?", even "what's wrong with you?"

But there are many universal hand gestures that can reveal what someone is feeling, as you engage with them. Throwing the hands up in the air is a universal expression of exasperation. Putting a hand in front of the body, with a straight arm is universally understood to mean "stop". But there are other ways the hands can tell us what's going on inside the people we engage with.

Gestures in which the palms are turned downward indicate

authority. With the arms outstretched, this type of gesture can also indicate a sense of superiority or domination. However, when the hands are used in gestures with the palms down, in the course of a conversation or business negotiation, the person gesturing is indicating an unwillingness to concede a point. When part of a firm, downward motion (like chopping), the message is "no".

Alternatively, gestures involving open palms indicate an earnest interest in reconciling a point, or a willingness to reach a concession or agreement. Palms facing up are an indication of openness.

Hands clenched in fists (unless you're about to engage in a fistfight), normally indicate discomfort and a sense of insecurity about the proceedings. When the thumb is tucked inside the fist, the person making this gesture is preparing themselves to confront a perceived threat and trying to strengthen themselves, in a completely unconscious way.

Placing the right hand over the heart is a sign that the person you're engaging is asking for your trust and wants to be believed. It's a gesture indicating sincerity. When consciously employed, it can be a ploy to deceive people into believing that the gesturer is sincere, when in fact, they're lying. This gesture is situational, but rooted in a desire to be believed.

Pointing at others is generally considered rude. When the

finger is jabbed, this gesture can be read as aggression. Generally, when people point in the course of a conversation, or when delivering a speech, the import is that of authority. The gesture denotes a command of the subject, as well as exhortation and a demand to be heard. Pointing can also provide emphasis (like a form of non-verbal punctuation).

Hands that appear to be squeezing or rubbing each other are a sign of nervousness, or self-pacification. This gesture can be seen in various forms, including lacing and unlacing the fingers, fiddling with rings or cuffs, or picking at the fingernails. The indication is that the gesturer is in a defensive stance and feels threatened or insecure in the context of the interaction.

When people place their hands on their hips, what they're doing physically is taking up more space. By physically magnifying their presence, they're establishing their authority and demanding that they be taken notice of. This is a dominant gesture and when accompanied by planted feet and erect posture, means nothing but business. The person with their hands on their hips (particularly if their hands are in fists) is telling you they are not in a mood for games. This is an "all business" gesture, indicating that the gesturer is uncompromising and not at all open to concessions or negotiations.

Placing the five digits of each hand together, at the fingertips, is called "steepling". While this gesture may easily be misread as conciliatory, what it's really transmitting is that the person making the gesture is inherently confident and authoritative. This is a person who can't be influenced, unless you have an extremely good rationale for whatever it is you're attempting to pitch. The "steepler" is a power player. When you see this hand gesture, you have met someone of considerable intellectual heft who can see through just about anyone.

## *Facial expressions*

The human face is an expressive collection of muscles that can tell you a great deal about people. Even the most apparently inscrutable people speak to others with their faces. In some cultures, this is more the truth than others. Some cultures are even known for a particular ability to conceal the emotions by controlling the face. Most of us, though, wear our emotions and opinions right on our faces, where the whole world can see them.

Most of us are capable of reading facial expressions only rather broadly. We know when someone's happy, because their smile tells us. We know when someone's angry, because the face contorts into an expression that is unpleasant. But there are many expressions the human face is capable of and these can be extraordinarily fleeting, remaining on the face for only from $1/15^{th}$ to $1/25^{th}$ of a second. That's not a lot of time to get a read. These brief expressions can reveal a lot about what we're thinking (and perhaps don't want to give away with our faces). Known as micro-expressions, there are seven to take note of. These are: contempt, disgust, fear, sadness, surprise, anger and happiness.

These expressions are seen on the faces of people all over the world. They transcend cultural and linguistic boundaries. They are even seen on the faces of those blind from birth and people who have never viewed television or other filmed media. This means that our facial expressions are deeply encoded in our human DNA. They are something we're born knowing how to do, like breathing. Recognizing these is a crucial in the project of learning to understand what people are thinking and feeling. As micro-expressions cross the face so rapidly, knowing the characteristics of each is helpful. Following are the hallmarks of each of the expressions listed:

**Disgust:** Something stinks! This is the expression your face will form, when that's the case. The nose wrinkles and as it does, the cheeks are pulled upward and the upper lip curls. Lines form under the eyes, as they're narrowed.

**Fear:** The mouth opens and the lips are drawn back, as both brows rise. As this happens, lines form in the forehead, vertically. The whites of the eyes show, above the iris.

**Surprise:** The jaw drops, as the mouth opens. The brows shoot up and lines form across the forehead, horizontally. The whites of the eyes show around the full circumference of the iris.

**Happiness:** As the corners of the mouth turn up, the

cheeks rise, the corners of the eyes crease and the lower lids become tense. Teeth may or may not be exposed. Genuine happiness is always indicated when lines form at the outer edges of the eyes. When this doesn't occur, happiness is being feigned.

**Anger:** As the jaw pushes out, the nostrils dilate. The mouth is tense, with the corners turning down. The brows are pulled together, with vertical lines forming between them. Eyes are fixed. For this expression to be completely readable as anger, all sectors of the face must be engaged.

**Contempt:** One side of the mouth is raised at the corner in the classical sneer. This expression may be accompanied by the rolling of the eyes.

**Sadness:** The lower lip is pushed outward and the corners of the mouth, pulled down. The eyebrows are pulled in, then drawn up. Of all the expressions listed in this section, this is the one least likely to be feigned effectively.

These are simple descriptions, but you can practice reproducing them, yourself. Stand in front of the mirror, attempting to match your facial expression to an emotion, without looking at the descriptions above. Now do the same, following the descriptions and paying attention to any differences you note. When you're aware of the subtleties of these expressions on your own face, you'll be more likely to catch them on the faces of others. These expressions can tell you a lot about the quality of a conversation you're having and the level of honesty being shared on the part of the person you're talking to.

# Chapter 4:  Tone and Pitch – Where Verbal meets Non-verbal

You can glean a lot of information from tone of voice.  When words are delivered in a certain tone and with a certain emphasis, they can take on different meanings.  For example, someone is inviting you to an event, but you sense that the invitation is offered grudgingly.  Why do you have that sensation?  It's the tone.  Does it seem half-hearted?  A resigned, or flat tone can indicate that the invitation is being recited in order to either please someone else, or out of social obligation.

Tone, pitch and even the cadence (rhythm) and speed of speaking can make the difference between being heard and being talked over.  You can also learn a lot about people's level of confidence from the rate of speed at which they speak.  The usual conversational pace is about 140 words per minute.   Faster than that and you're perceived to be prattling.  Slower than that and you'll either have people hanging on your every word (the current American President comes to mind), or bored to death.

Tone of voice completely changes the message, as we've discussed above. In the popular television show, Seinfeld, when the character, Neuman (who is not well-loved by other characters on the show) appears, the refrain is "Hello, Neuman". But the tone of voice this is delivered in is uniformly venomous. Less a greeting, than a threat! Tone can convey subtext by transforming words in rather surprising ways.

For women readers, this is especially important. Tone and pitch must be carefully modulated, particularly in business circles. Lowering the pitch of your voice causes your words to change in terms of value to the listener, particularly when you're talking to men. Men are known to "zone out" at times, when women speak. It's therefore incredibly important that women modulate their voices, speaking in a manner which commands the attention of others, when you desire to so command it. For women, this is a form of linguistic mirroring. Because the tone of male voices tends to be lower than that of most women, buy mirroring that tonal quality, a sleight of hand is performed in which women may mirror their male fellows and demand that they listen.

The human voice is like an instrument. You are in control of it and you decide how it's going to sound. If you're hoping to draw a listener or listeners in, drop the volume. Slow down. Watch them lean in. Vary the tonal quality of what you're saying, adding emphasis at the end of a sentence to add a question mark (which most of us do naturally), or lowering it to impart authority to your words. Pause, if you need to.

Consider what will come next. If you've taken the time to compose a thought and believe that it's worth listening to, have the confidence not to blurt. Take as much time delivering the thought in words as you've spent composing it.


A fascinating aspect of the quality of people's voices is that they can tell us a lot about the people speaking. Everyone has a vocal quality that is habitual, to some extent. Often, we're unaware of it. Some people sound whiny and nasal, without even knowing it. Others sound warm and effusive, by nature. Then, some folks have a flat, monotonous quality to their voices. Sometimes, culture and language can effect tone and pitch. Usually, though, tone and pitch imply an attitude that is unspoken, but evident. Paying attention to the quality of people's voices and the sensation experienced when you hear them will train your ears to factor voice into your evaluation of those around you.


Remember, they may be doing the same with you. It's important that you're aware of how you sound. You may want to practice reading out loud to get a sense of how you sound to others. You can video or record yourself and play it back. How do you sound to yourself? What mannerisms are you displaying for others to read? What is your face saying? Getting a read on yourself is a good foundation for applying your self-knowledge to your interpretation of those around you. When you're able to take an objective look at the signals you're sending, you'll be better able to read them in others.

## Dress and aesthetics

If you invited someone to your wedding and they showed up in flip flops, sweatpants and a baseball cap, as if they had just been shopping in their local grocery store, or had rolled out of bed and not even showered, what would be your conclusion? You would probably conclude that this person did not care about your wedding and was, very likely, not happy to be there. What other conclusion could be drawn?

A persons sartorial and personal care habits are visible signs of their attitudes toward themselves and others. Particularly in the workplace, a lackadaisical approach to one's appearance can indicate a lack of concern for the quality of the work, the standards of the workplace, or both. People who present themselves well look confident, because they feel confident. Their hair is groomed. Their clothing is attractive, clean and presentable and their nails are clean. They know they look good. Those who tend not to care very much about the details of presentation tend not to be perceived as competent and perhaps as suffering from low self-esteem.

So it's extremely important that you send the right message to others by presenting yourself as one who deems appearance to be of some importance. That is not to say that everyone's expected to be a preening peacock, as that style of presentation can be just as distracting (if not, more so) than neglect. Whether we choose to admit it or not, people tend to judge others on their appearance and if yours isn't well-curated, or curated at all, with no concession to public standards, you will not be well-regarded.

As I've said above, a lack of concern for personal appearance can indicate a number of realities under the surface, but sometimes, looks are deceiving. People who tend not to care a great deal about their appearance can be intensely intellectual and engaged in their work. This is particularly true of computer programmers, academics and others involved in work that involves a high level of focus. There's more to some people than meets the eye, so it's always wise to factor in variables when reaching an evaluation. As you'll know if you've read this far, knowing about people is about a lot of little things – not just one big thing.

As for you, this section will have made clear the kind of message that's genuinely appealing – pride in one's appearance. That's expressed by an overall attention to grooming and appropriateness of dress. A sense of style is a bonus. If you don't have one, spend some time thinking about how those you admire present themselves and ask yourself how you might create that effect yourself. If you lack a lot of savvy in that department, remember to keep it simple, streamlined and tidy. This will send the message that you care, are confident about yourself, but also professional. That's probably the most important factor, especially for those of you reading who hope to learn the skills involved in developing influential gifts. First impressions are lasting impressions. You can be the smartest man or woman in the room, but if you look like an unmade bed, it won't matter one bit.

All the factors listed are elements of communication. Everything you say, do and wear, every expression on your face, every gesture and every high and low in the tone and pitch of your voice tells a tale about what you intend. Knowing how to honestly evaluate yourself in all these departments is a solid way of developing your influential heft. When you know yourself and your habits and can objectively see them as elements of your own communicative style, knowing you can improve some or all of them, you'll be better equipped to influence others. By deconstructing your own style, you'll have a window into how others are communicating with you, using all these elements.

Lance Burdett, a communications professional who has worked as National Advisor to the New Zealand Police Crisis Negotiation Teams, says that the importance of effective communication can't be overstated. He is well known for his insistence that effective communication can diffuse anger and correct abusive behavior. He says that good communication skills (including evaluation of the communication styles of others), are the basis for an ability to defuse potentially dangerous situations, and to help reduce the toxicity of potentially explosive environments. It is, for example, very tempting to react with anger when someone speaks to you angrily. But does that get you where you want to be in terms of advancing your agenda? Nothing could be further from the truth. Having the ability to measure your response, especially in tense situations, can be crucial to a satisfactory outcome. Finesse and attention to detail are key in situations in which anger can turn to violence in a heartbeat. How effective these skills are in your everyday life is highlighted by their importance in police work, when their successful application can mean life or death.

By understanding social psychology and having the requisite inter-personal skills, you have the ability to meet people where they stand and to appeal to what matters to them. Having the skill of being able to effectively read and interpret the communicative clues people send us, both verbally and non-verbally, is the basis for social and professional success.

Following is a brief summary of making your spoken communication more effective and clear:

## *Be specific*

Say what you mean. Mean what you say. Ensure that the message others receive is the one you intend and that your gestures, expressions, body language and tone match. There should be no perceived dissonance between these various elements of your communicative style, but when you speak with conviction and honesty, that won't be a problem. Before you can convince others, or influence them, you have to buy what you're selling, yourself. You're your first best or worst customer. Be sure of your message and be sure it's clear, concise and keyed to the person or people you're talking to, in order to find the common ground you seek.

## Read the signs

Good communication is a matter of persuasion, not force. Do not, for example, try to convince yourself that the listener is fully engaged with the conversation in order to flatter yourself. Sometimes people are just being polite and trying not to offend you. They may be bored, offended, or tired. Pay attention to the expressions and body language of those you're talking to. Don't be a bore. It is imperative that you work on understanding the art of non-verbal communication so that you can take an accurate reading of whatever situation you are in. Proficiency in understanding people's behavior in social interactions is key to navigating them successfully. Knowing who you're talking to is of vital importance. While you may have grand ideas about the value of what you're saying, watch the listener to ensure you're not deluding yourself.

## Exercise critical thinking and sound judgment

Thinking critically, more than anything else, is about reading beneath the surface and drilling down to the core of whatever is under discussion. If someone is telling you that proposition "A" is the truth and that it's been duly vetted, considered and has buy in, do you take this statement at face value, or do you ensure that this is the case? Even with your own propositions – have you fully convinced yourself that you're entirely on board, or are you fudging it, because you want to believe you're correct?

Critical thinking is a process that precludes assumptions and a willingness to take things at face value. It demands more of you, in terms of applying a judicious and objective reading of people, situations and events. It further demands that you be willing to call yourself out at times when you haven't taken the time to obtain all the facts you need prior to making an agreement, adopting a stance, or taking an action. In essence, critical thinking is the opposite of being "reactionary" (acting solely on instinct, uninformed by intellectual understanding). Critical thinking and the sound judgment that flows from its exercise is key to effective communication. What you discover, in the process of critical thought, is a 360 degree view of the truth, in its fullness. This allows you to identify contingencies, worst case scenarios and any other possible consequences of making certain decisions, statement or agreements.

While critical thinking can't always prevent things happening that you'd rather not happen, it can work as a type of prophylactic against making errors that needn't be made, in most instances. Thinking critically implies seeing things for what they are, in all their facets. That includes the reading of people. You may look at certain people in certain ways, but are those ways critically informed? Have you asked yourself what the emotional basis for their words and actions are? Are you, in fact, being fair?

In approaching interpersonal communication from a critical standpoint, you're able to apply the knowledge you gain from a critical reading of people to arrive at the best outcome, for all involved, without prejudice.

# Chapter 5:  The Joy of Influence

Are you happy when people believe what you say? If you are, then you'll be happy to hear there's a way of achieving this effect systematically, through the cultivation of understanding the non-verbal, physical cues which form your perceptions of other people and vice versa. Are you happy when people stop what they're doing to pay attention to what you have to say? Obviously, it is a sign they think you're worth listening to. That's why judges and House Speakers use the gavel to call for silence and attention. Sometimes people are distracted, fidgety and unwilling to collect themselves long enough to listen (particularly politicians trying to get re-elected seated in legislative chambers).

We've discussed some the various factors involved in communication in the previous chapter.  All these factors add up to whether communication is effective or not.  You're not the Speaker of the House.  You have no gavel.  So it's important that you're able to communicate effectively. Slamming things on the table might get people's attention, but that's not the type of attention you're looking for. You need to send the message that you are worth listening to. People who are worth listening to convey a certain sense of self which is rooted in confidence. That message is sent via all the verbal and non-verbal clues we give others. Our understanding of where our weaknesses and strengths lie can inform a better understanding of those same qualities in others.

## *Authority and Influence*

Authority and influence are two entirely different things. To be honest, I'd rather be in a position of influence that one of authority. Influence is subtle. Authority is obvious. Influence is covert. Authority is overt. As an influencer, you have much more latitude then you might in a position of authority, because people in positions of authority are bound by the conventions of that same authority. For instance, a government leader may want to enact legislation, but is unable to, due to a fractious legislative body. But lobby groups, citizens' groups and non-governmental organizations can wield great influence in moving that fractious legislative body and getting the job done. Authority does a good job of looking powerful, but influence is the little man behind the curtain, actually getting things done.

To wield influence, it's not necessary to be in a position of authority or power for this reason. Influence is like the water that eventually erodes stone – subtle and unseen, but very real. While authority may well be the Hulk. Influence is the

Ninja, stalking its objectives with determination, consistency and persistent dedication. Influential skill is a very desirable aptitude to cultivate for this reason.

The Center for Creative Leadership has established that influence has three essential components and an accompanying set of tactics: emotion, logic and cooperation. The first of these is probably the most accessible road to influence, as people's emotional lives are very close to the surface, most of the time. Appealing to the those you want to enlist to your cause via their emotions involves expressing your own conviction about whatever that cause is and moreover, expressing a belief that they have a pivotal part to play in the realization of your vision.

To make an effective emotional appeal, your powers of communicative interpretation come to the forefront. Who are you appealing to? Knowing this is key to effectively mounting an appeal rooted in emotion. What are the person's values and beliefs? What goals is this person shooting for and how can you help them get there? How does your vision uphold all these emotional factors and honor them? Being keenly aware of the values of the person you're talking to and how you can weave those values into your vision is how you build support using an influential emotional appeal.

Appealing to someone's logic involves showcasing the benefits of your vision to the organization or group and also, the person you're appealing to. A strong case built on logic will be accompanied by concrete evidence that your cause is not only viable, but desirable, in terms of implementation. This tactical style of influence demands that you be intimately connected with the nuts and bolts of your vision and passionate about influencing others to support it. Be fully prepared to defend your vision against objections by reading your plan, or idea through the eyes of a critic. Your critical deconstruction of your vision is a crucial part of the success of a logical appeal.

Positive team-building can result from a well-crafted cooperative appeal, in which you outline a plan or project in terms of mutual support and benefit. Creating a consultative framework for all parties to involve themselves in implementation is highly effective as a way of building influence. As you put people to work, you display confidence in their abilities. This creates strong networks of influence, as people don't forget those who've given them opportunities. They also don't forget strong leadership that results in effective action. By applying a cooperative appeal in support of a vision or project, you're not only realizing your goal, but you're undergirding your influence. From the process, it's inevitable that you will also grow new thought leaders for your organization, which is nothing but positive and casts you as a visionary.

Effective influence combines all three strategies concurrently and builds organizational confidence in your abilities. Where authority can prescribe, influence can actually fill the prescription. The doctor may pull down the big bucks, but the pharmacist delivers the cure.

So wielding influence is about building networks, knowing who you're talking to and being capable of providing logical and compelling reasons for what you have in mind. In learning to build your influential power, you're engaging your powers of communicative interpretation, emotional intelligence and critical thinking. All these factors, in the practice of influence, are hallmarks of leadership. In developing these skills, you're becoming a more well-rounded person and a force to be reckoned with.

## *Modelling Excellence*

Influence is also inherent in your actions, your demeanor and your treatment of other people. Your work habits, your attention to detail, your presentation and your likeability all work together. They make you someone who is capable of wielding influence in any situation or organization. All these factors are just as important as your messaging, your knowledge and training and your people-reading skills.

People want to work with those they like. They want to spend their (at least) eight hours per day, five days per week, around people they find easy to get along with, helpful and cooperative. That's the bare minimum. If you're hoping to develop your influence in the workplace, then it goes without saying that you need to go the extra mile when it comes to modelling excellence.

Excellent employees don't just come in to work on time and leave a little late. They're not just willing to help and cooperate. Excellent employees see details others don't. They tie up loose ends, volunteer for projects others aren't necessarily interested in and help to create an environment of harmonious efficiency and genial collegiality. These are the foundations of excellence. Out of that foundation grows the solid stuff of organizational integrity, built by quality work that is doing a lot more than collecting a pay check. It's building something as part of a team and intentionally so.

How excellence is modelled is in the details many overlook. Excellent employees sweat that (apparently) small stuff, because they know it matters. Excellence is a collection of minutia that culminates in a whole. Your mood in the workplace. Your reputation among your peers. The quality of your work. The quality of your interactions. Your place on the team. Your consistency and commitment. These are all components of excellence and they're worthy of emulation. That's why others will emulate it. Those who aren't interested in doing so – who watch with jaded, envious eyes as excellence builds its influential power - are of no consequence. They're not interested and that won't go unnoticed when push comes to shove, or downsizing comes to town. What matters is that you're being the change you want to see. Modelling excellence means making yourself an icon of your vision and its soundness. This is what gets you heard, noticed and influencing those around you.

## Client care excellence

You are likely to retain clients who feel you understand them even when they aren't particularly communicative, verbally. It is a sign they feel that you have internalized their needs, when, with just a gesture or two, they can let you know where they're at. This also fosters a sense of familiarity and collegiality that inspires customer loyalty. They will feel that you value them, because it's clear you can read them well. In short, by being able to perceive your clients' non-verbal communication, you endear yourself to them and make of yourself a trusted friend. Likewise, you need to be understood by them without either party having to resort to long emails or sitting through endless, time-wasting meetings. Solid business relationships are all about ease of communication and communal satisfaction with their quality. Being able to read the non-verbal cues offered by your clients can set you apart as an intuitive, savvy leader.

When excellence is inherent in your work and communications style, it will typify your client relationships. This is undeniable. The same excellence you model in your day to day work flows into the client relationship, strengthening it and sustaining it in a world of competitive challengers. Client care is what sets the best apart. As always, God is in the details. Understanding client need is rooted in understanding the client, the rhythms of the business involved, branding, budgeting and human resources. All of this information is your business and having a strong command of it, as well as an open and communicative relationship with your clients, can set you well apart. You are there when needed and you are effective.

Excellent custom care amounts to a sense of service, a word too seldom heard. It should be your very favorite word when it comes to your clients, even if those clients who are internal (your co-workers).

Some minor factors to consider which may sometimes elude us amount to social niceties that also count as body language. These are forms of communication that continue to be important, regardless of their diminished cultural significance in some circles. It's important to understand the following information about engagement in the course of business interactions. These are professional interactions, not personal ones. For that reason, please read the following as a proviso against entirely preventable faux pas. Little slips in such seemingly inconsequential areas may seem excusable, but they can cost you valuable influence that you're trying to build up, not tear down. They matter.

## *Firm handshake*

Have you ever thought about what a firm handshake says to your current or potential client? A firm, confident handshake sends the message that you're resolved and in control. Even today, the message of a firm handshake is that of competence and reliability. It means business, in the most basic sense. There was a day, not so very long ago, when women in business (who were rare), didn't extend their hands to be shaken by male business people. Women simply operated on a different level than men did in those times. These days, though, women are expected to similarly deliver a strong, confident handshake, which does not linger unduly, but is not retracted suddenly, as though being snatched from a fiery furnace. There's a happy medium.

Take care with being overly familiar with clients you don't know. Adding a hand on the shoulder, or a pat on the back is for those you know well. It's not for the client you've just signed on. Knowing when such additional non-verbal communication is appropriate is part of being able to read the bones of interpersonal niceties, especially in business.

## Eye contact – handle with care

Making direct eye contact sends the message that you are genuinely interested in what the other person is saying. Of course, you should assess the length and intensity of the gaze. Sustained eye contact can be read as intimidation, or even sexual interest, so it's important that you look away occasionally, punctuating the action with a nod of the head, or other accompanying mannerisms to ensure it's not misunderstood as diminished interested.

# Chapter 6: Techniques for Effective Communication

You are at an advantage when you can communicate effectively. After all, you are the person who knows your goals and how you hope to achieve them. The point is that you are not going to achieve those goals single-handedly, because you don't live in isolation. Every single one of us needs allies, friends and supporters along the way. How do you work with other people unless you can get your point across? How can you develop strong and lasting allegiances unless you understand what's going on with the people you work with?

Earlier we discussed building influence and how you can achieve that through a variety of strategic devices, as well as being someone who models excellence in all you do. Now we'll look at some other techniques to support what we've already learned.

Following are some useful psychological techniques that help in effective communication:

## Neuro-linguistic Programming (NLP)

Created in the 1970s by two California doctors (Drs. Bandler and Grinder), neuro-linguistic programming is a method employing theories of psychoanalysis and communication, toward helping people develop themselves more fully. NLP advances the idea that many of our behaviors are programmed and can be altered for the better, due to a link through linguistic and neurological realities. There are strong links between what we do, what we say and how we behave that Drs. Bandler and Grinder believed, in developing NLP, could be useful for the modification of undesirable or socially unviable behaviors. They further believed that these alterations would result in dramatic improvements in the quality of the relationships and professional lives of those who used these techniques.

NLP's goal is to understand how the human mind perceives things; how to use all your senses comprehensively to effectively send your intended message through verbal and non-verbal communication. NLP can also help you apply this understanding in order to communicate more effectively, by creating rapport between you and other people. Needless to say, how you present yourself and what you have to say matters a lot, with regard to the way others perceive you. When our neuro-linguistic patterning provokes behaviors that prevent effective communication, this can be "re-patterned" in order to deliver better results.

Does it mean you are failing if you can't persuade someone to change their mind, or budge on a dearly held position?

The answer is no. It just means you need a bit of personal tweaking. As we've discussed throughout this book, part of that has to do with understanding yourself and how you present to others. It also has to do with applying that knowledge to your own perceptions about other people. But when it comes to our behaviors (some of which have to do with non-verbal language), perhaps NLP is the silver bullet to more successful and fruitful interactions with other people. With your sharpened communication skills, you will still be fostering a constructive work environment, because NLP is helpful in doing that by virtue of the following characteristics:

- Helps you communicate clearly.

- Helps you have a positive personal impact on people.

- Helps you build trust among colleagues and friends.

- Helps you put people at ease and by doing so, elicit sincere reactions and feedback from them.

- Helps you build respect among colleagues and friends.

- Helps you appreciate other people's point of view, even when it differs from your own.

- Helps you use the existing climate to bring about your preferred outcome.

And what is the result of using the NLP technique?

- Your workplace team can reiterate what you have communicated to them correctly and mirror your intentions, ensuring they deliver the outcomes you desire.

- You provide your team with the opportunity to express their opinions, even when they differ from your own. This tension is healthy and encourages creative dissent, which can build the team through confidence in your leadership and in the validity of team opinions.

- Your technique can enhance the impact of your verbal message, serving a complementary role. For example, a pat on the back, delivered in concert with a verbal message of approval for a job well done, has a reinforcing effect, which complements the spoken message.

- You can underline your verbal message, when you throw your hands in the air as you verbalize your exasperation. That is called "accenting".

All of these changes in your communications style are possible with NLP. Of course, seeking out a trained professional to assist you with the process is highly recommended. If you feel that resorting to clinical help is necessary to help you succeed in life in places where you have gotten "stuck", it's well worth considering.

## Self-Hypnosis

Just for clarification, this technique has nothing to do with the "Svengali effect", in which a stage hypnotist attempts to overwhelm your personal autonomy; inducing you to submit to his charismatic control. Life is not a movie. Here you are not going to learn how to put anyone in a trance.

This technique is concerned with fostering effective communication by encouraging your mind to work at a higher, level. You will learn to clear out distracting thoughts arising from your environment and to delve deeply into your thought processes. By following this technique, you can come to understand what you want and how you intend to go about getting it. You will also learn to decipher non-verbal cues you have noted in your interactions with others, providing you with an objective reading of all factors in any given situation. This process can enhance your objectivity and improve your ability to make rationally-informed and sound decisions.

In short, self-hypnosis helps you achieve the following:

- Avoid distractions and improve concentration.

- Solve problems by having a better and more well-rounded understanding of them.

- Formulate ideas as part of a strategic plan you can then put into practice.

Taking the time to train your mind to be quiet and to make space for rapid analysis and evaluation is a worthwhile pursuit. It may sound a little unorthodox, but making it possible for your brain to make decisions based on careful analysis, instead of being alive with detritus that's not serving you in the project of moving forward with your life is something which can genuinely make you more effective in every area of your life. Self-hypnosis can help you achieve this.

# Chapter 7: Using NLP to Manage People

When it comes to managing people effectively, it's important that you first understand the non-verbal cues they provide, in order to be able to apply your skills toward influencing them. This is an important principle in applying the NLP technique. Following are a few NLP techniques that can allow you to influence people's perception and thinking:

## *Deciphering eye movements*

The reason it is important to understand the meaning of eye movements is that each eye movement tells its own tale. For instance, when you're searching for the right word, or trying to remember a name, you automatically move your eyes in a certain way (most likely, squinting). Rolling the eyes signals contempt, or exasperation. Winking indicates flirtation, or a joke. Widening the eyes signals surprise, or shock; even extreme excitement. We've discussed earlier, how eye movements are also implicated in other facial expressions.

In fact, the eyes can reveal much more about people's mental and emotional status, all on their own.

Once you understand what other people's thought processes are, you can accurately follow a course of action or dialogue which acknowledges the unspoken response, as signaled by the eyes. And as you may know, eye movements complement other forms of communication such as hand movements, speech and, as stated elsewhere in this book and above, facial expressions. Dilation of the pupils, breathing, angle of the body, position of the hands – all these are complementary to the spoken message. Still, eye movement is very important in communication, because every movement is influenced by particular senses, as well as different parts of the brain.

Here is how you can generally interpret eye movement:

### Visual responsiveness

- Eyes upward, then towards the right:

Whenever a person tilts eyes upward and then to the right, it means that the person is formulating a mental picture.

- Eyes upward, then towards the left:

Whenever a person tilts eyes upward, followed by an eye movement to the left, it means the person is recalling a certain image.

• Eyes looking straight ahead:

Whenever someone focuses directly in front of them, as though looking at a point in the distance, this indicate that the person is not focused on anything in particular. That is the look often referred to as 'glazed'.

## *Auditory Responsiveness.*

• Eyes looking towards the right:

When a person's eyes shift straight towards the right, it means the person is in the process of constructing a sound.

• Eyes looking towards the left:

When a person's eyes shift straight towards the left, it indicates that the person is recalling a sound.

## *Audio-digital responsiveness*

• Eyes looking downward, then switching to the left:

When someone drops their eyes and then proceeds to turn their eyes to the left, this signals that the person is engaged in internal dialogue.

• Eyes looking right down then left to right:

When a person looks downward and then proceeds to turn their eyes to the left and then, to the right in consecutive movements, it means the person is engaged in negative self-talk.

## *Kinesthetic responsiveness:*

Here, the person looks directly down, only to turn the eyes to the right. That is an indication that the person is evaluating emotional status. This further indicates

that the person is not at ease.

## *Verbal responses:*

Rhythmic speech

The idea here is not to be poetic as you speak, but to speak at a regular pace. The recommended pace of speaking is equated to the heartbeat, say, between 45 and 72 beats per minute. At that pace, you are likely to sustain the listener's attention and establish greater receptivity to what you're saying. While normal conversational speed averages about 140 words per minute, slowing down a little and taking time to pause is highly effective as a means of sustaining people's attention. Your regular cadence should be punctuated by fluctuations in tone and emphasis, in order not to sound monotonous.

Repeating key words

When you are trying to influence someone, there are key words or phrases which that carry additional weight as far as your message is concerned. This method of speaking is a way of embedding the message in the listener and subtly suggesting that your message is valid and worthy of reception. Repeating key words also suggests commitment, conviction and mastery of the subject matter.

Using strongly suggestive language

Use language that is positive and supportive of what you are saying, using a selection set of strong, descriptive words or phrases. As you do this, you should observe the person you are speaking to closely, in a way that makes them feel as though you are seeing right through them and aware of what they are thinking. Don't be invasive about this, or aggressive. Merely suggest, by way of your gaze that you have a keen appreciation of what makes people tick. This places you in a dominant position, especially when accompanied by dominant body language, like "steepling" (see section on hand gestures). It helps to use suitable, complementary body language as you speak, to subtly underscore the message.

Touching the person lightly, as you speak

Touching the person as you speak to them draws their attention to you in a relaxed and familiar way. By employing this technique, you're preparing the listener to absorb what you are saying to them; a way of programming attentiveness. Those engaging in inter-gender conversations in the workplace should take great care with this technique, as it can lead to misunderstandings.

Using a mixture of "hot" and "vague" words

"Hot" words are those that tend to provoke specific sensations in the listener. When you are using them to influence someone's thinking, it is advisable to use them in a suitable pattern. Examples of phrases containing hot words are: *it means; feel free; see this; because; hear this.* The effect of employing these words and phrases is that you're directing influencing the listener's state of mind, including how that person feels, imagines and perceives. You're also appealing to the sense most prevalent in the listener's perceptive style (as observed through the movement of their eyes). For example, the phrase "hear this" will appeal to those who indicate a tendency to respond most actively to auditory stimuli.

## Using the interspersal technique

The interspersal technique is the practice of stating one thing, while hoping to impress on the listener something entirely different. For example, you could make a positive statement like:

*John is very generous, <u>but</u> some people take advantage of him and treat him as though he is gullible.*

When someone hears this statement, the likely assumption is that you want people to appreciate John's generosity. That is likely to be the message heard and yet, the subtext is that while John is generous, he is also considered gullible and thus, at a disadvantage in life, when it comes to other people. Your hidden agenda may be to influence the listener to actually think of John as gullible, which calls into question his judgment. So emphasize the words "but" and "gullible". The word "but" serves the purpose of transitioning the perceived compliment to John to an implicit slight.

The techniques just described form strategies in the service of influencing people. They're not intended to force a viewpoint, or to control people's behavior for nefarious ends.

These techniques are intended to modify undesirable behaviors which may be resulting in workplace difficulties, including the failure of staff to work well together, or to complete team projects. They're also extremely helpful in the context of relationships with young people and children, whether at home, or in a learning environment. Techniques of subtle manipulative effect like those described, though capable of influencing people and their behavior, don't amount to anything even approaching coercion. The person being spoken to chooses all responses and is merely influenced, or steered toward those responses.

# Chapter 8: Combining Hypnosis and NLP in Communication

## *Understanding the Human Mind*

To be able to choose the best tool of communication in any circumstance, you need to be in a position to understand the workings of the human mind. Then you can proceed to evaluate the tools at your disposal to see which are best suited to your attempts at persuasion.

First of all, we're all gathering abundant information from non-verbal clues in the course of our daily lives, whether we're aware it's happening, or not. Being aware of the information we're gathering renders it useful and helpful. All this information is stored in your mind. However, since your mind is just like a computer and can crash from the intensity of too much data, it stores a lot of that information in its 'archives', only to retrieve it when required. The retrieved information is then programmed in your mind's sub-conscious. From there, it influences your responses and behavior in ways you may not always understand, if you're unaware.

## *Hypnosis and NLP*

When it comes to hypnosis and NLP, both are effective tools of communication, and particularly persuasion, yet their approaches to communication are different. However, when you are trying to influence someone, these complement each other very well, as communication tools. They both have powerful effects on the sub-conscious, the level of the mind in which information processing and programming takes place.

What happens with hypnosis and also NLP, is that you present suggestions to the person you are trying to influence; suggestions intended for the person's unconscious mind. This means your intentions at the point of communication are not explicit or obvious to the person you are communicating with. Yet you succeed in embedding that information in the person's unconscious mind. That information is available for retrieval as you continue giving your well-tailored suggestions. It's then programmed into the person's sub-conscious in a way that influences their actions to suit your intentions.

It's time to dispel the misguided notion that hypnosis and NLP are tricky gimmicks intended to manipulate people into abandoning their free will. You need to see both techniques as tools that can help you influence people by restructuring the process of their thinking. Hypnosis, a tool that's feared by many, derives its effectiveness from helping to induce in the subject a state of awareness that is more heightened than usual. That is why you are able to reach the person's sub-conscious and influence a change of behavior, through a change in the way think and therefore, perceive.

### *In simple terms, what is hypnosis and what is NLP?*

### Hypnosis

- Hypnosis is both a state of mind and a process of communication.

- It is all natural – not induced by anything chemical. It's completely safe.

- Hypnosis may be carried out verbally, with a hypnotist uttering words which embed in the subject a change in behavior (quitting smoking, for only one example). In other instances, it is predominantly visual. At other times, hypnosis may be driven by auditory stimuli.

- With hypnosis, the subject remains fully aware of their particular surroundings. In short, it's not true that hypnosis subjects are under a trance, or experience anything very far removed from normal consciousness.

• Hypnosis induces deep concentration that focuses subjects so profoundly, that external suggestions are more readily accepted.

• It is a technique that has been proven, scientifically, to help in accelerating changes in human behavior.

• It is a state of mind in which subjects remain fully alert and focused Hypnosis is not sleep, even though that's what suggested by the word's Greek origins. In reality, the process of hypnosis involves a deep level of concentration, enhanced relaxation and more ready reception of suggestion, as well as expectation.

• While in the hypnotic state, the subject's focus is guided by selective thinking, so that the practitioner establishes a desired behavioral or perceptive change.

• The process of hypnosis bypasses critical thinking. This is how hypnosis works to arrive at an understanding on the part of the subject that the suggestion provided is valid. The subject of hypnosis does not critically analyze the suggestion because the left side of the brain, which is in charge of analyzing information, switches off during hypnosis, leaving only the right side of the brain working and in an enhanced state of attentiveness.

- Hypnosis is an easy tool to use and you don't need any special talent to be able to apply it in effective communication. Research has shown that 90% of people can be successfully hypnotized. History teaches that there are many leaders who have managed to hypnotize people with words and complementary body language. Some of these leaders have used this ability to nefarious ends, but hypnosis is a tool that can be used to provoke desirable behavioral change toward positive goals.

**NLP**

- NLP is a modern science concerned with human behavior. It is becoming more popular and widely practiced by the day, owing to its effectiveness in improving social interactions, work environments, and many other spheres in which people interact.

- NLP is based on the belief that language affects communication and subsequently affects behavior.

- NLP is based on techniques formulated by Milton Erickson, a very influential hypnotherapist and psychologist and also a pioneer in family therapy.

- It is a system that involves identifying behavioral patterns toward their modification. Its impact is quite rapid compared to other persuasion techniques.

- People who employ NLP as a way of improving a variety of personal competence and skill are often those with a clear vision about what they want to achieve in their chosen field.

- Today, fields embracing NLP as a tool for improvement include athletics, health, education, business, personal development and professional development.

- NLP is about making the environment comfortable for the subject and also safe for everyone involved, encouraging subjects to respond rapidly and effectively.

- It is not a detached scientific theorem, but which is abundantly evidenced in daily human behavior. For example, a salesperson competent in NLP is able to succeed in his or her career, by following NLP's step by step process, based on the five senses. Such a salesperson is able to build rapport with the client because of an ability to detect when a buyer has unspoken objections and further, how to overcome those objections by appealing to the subject profiled a tailored communicative style.

- NLP not only leads to people adjusting their attitudes, it also leads to productive and positive changes to problematic behaviors.

# Chapter 9: Practical Influence

Allan Cohen and David Bradford are the co-authors of the book, *Influence Without Authority*. As discussed earlier in this book, authority and influence are two very different animals. Some believe that authority is the key driver of change, but my contention (and that of the authors of the book) is that it's possible to effect real change with influence, without having any actual authority.

Their work focuses on some key components of learning how to influence people in positions that wield more power than the one you are in. This applies to bosses, political leaders, or anyone who is recognized as authoritative by virtue of their position. Knowing what matters to people who've climbed a little higher up the ladder than you, without having to resort to political machinations (which can be dangerous and even destructive), is key to being able to do this. Creating partnerships with people in positions of authority is also a key influential skill. Having something to offer them which appeals to their core values and interests (discussed earlier in this book), while having a logical framework to support your ability to achieve these kinds of partnerships.

## Mutual Respect

Forming partnerships has everything to do with reciprocity. Scratching someone's back should result in an equal and opposite reaction (scratching yours), if mutual respect is present in the relationship. If you show your employees contempt, it's understandable that they mirror that contempt by not giving a hoot about what happens to your business, beyond getting their wages. The best way to influence people positively is to treat them with respect. You may not know your employees at a personal level and may not really know what they are capable of. By the same token, not honoring your role in the organization, whether it stems from a resentment for authority, or a simple neglect, is disrespectful. You won't form any partnerships if you're not modelling personal excellence that's measurable and visible.

Learning who people are and what their ethical universes are like is the first step to being able to influence them. Personal interactions are based on building your knowledge of individual personalities and interacting with each person you know, live with or work with on their level. This is only possibly when it's pursued from a genuine interest in people and leaders all have that going for them.

***Situations where this influence model is most effective:***

- When you have no authority over someone, but need their help.

- When you are dealing with a person who is disinclined to help.

- When you have no goodwill or friendship with the person from whom you need help.

- When you hardly know the person you want to solicit help from.

***How to Carry Out the Reciprocity Model of Influence***

*Develop the notion that everyone is potentially helpful*

Everyone around you is a potential ally. This should go without saying, but in a hierarchically-based society, we tend to overlook people who aren't decision-makers, gatekeepers, or somehow part of the top tier of whatever enterprise we're involved in. Everyone around you is not only worthy of your respect, but potentially someone with information, entrée, or other supportive ballast. Life is a matter of seeing other people as part of your personal support network. That's a mutual thing. Remember that as you move forward. Allies work together. It's also important to think of the world as a deeply interconnected place, in which someone you know knows someone you need to know. Sooner or later, the goodwill you spread all around you, evident in the network you'll build because of that goodwill, will render a connection that's going to bear abundant fruit. By the same token, ill will can spread just as rapidly and break important connections, cutting you off from potential allies. Keep that mind, each and every day and remember that you're only as connected as your most recent connection suggests (and that one should have been made the last time you went out the door).

By having this positive outlook, you avoid being anxious as you approach people to enlist their help or support. You also become well-liked and pleasant to be around and people (of course) love that. Seeing that you're willing to make an approach encourages people to lend you their ear and consider you and your ideas with an open mind. It also means your intelligence network grows, because every single person you meet is a fountain of information. With that network growth, your reputation as a person of integrity and honesty grows.

*Have your priorities straight*

Constantly demanding that other people come around to your way of thinking is not going to build your relationships. It's going to tear them down. If you're seen as single mindedly focused on achieving personal goals, you'll be viewed as the type of relentless, Type A jerk most people don't want to be around. Subtlety is the watchword ever in your mind. Maintain your network through genuine friendship and allegiance and you won't need to be that way. You'll find that people just agree with you because they like you. Being personable and easy to be around is the best possible strategy for getting things done the way you want them done. This is a well-known fact. People want to work with people they like. Being liked and admired is always the best way to build a support system and a sterling reputation that will bring you into the presence of those who can help and support your ideas and your goals.

Ultimately, then, your first priority is the cultivation of strong, reliable relationships with those around you. These will stand you in good stead.

*Who's who?*

It is important that you understand, for example, if the person whose opinion you are seeking has a personal relationship with the business owner, or the Chief Executive of the enterprise you're involved in. You may wish to seek a second opinion if you realize, for instance, that the CEO is this person's brother or golf buddy. At the same time, knowing what sort of relationships are in play is part of building your network. It's important to understand the dynamics of your workplace and the relationships involved. That's more than possible when your network is built on trust in you and your integrity. If anyone in that network suspects you can't be trusted, it's likely many will – even all. Again, this will bring it all crashing down.

By building a support network, you will be offered reams of useful information - historical grudges, friendships, business missteps, human resources traffic – all these factors can provide you with a clear picture of the people in play and who your strongest and most influential allies might be. Somewhere in that network is the wormhole through time and space – the one that opens the doors you wish to be opened.

*Be clear in your communications*

It is important that you be clear what you need from others so that they understood exactly what's being asked of them. If you are not clear, you could have a long discussion and even share meals together and yet end up with nothing that moves your cause forward. Even if this is what shakes out from your explorations, you're still spending your time well, as you're learning about an ally and what gets them interested and keeps them interested. You're learning about that person's goals, dreams and aptitudes and this is all useful information. Further, it places you in a mentoring position, which permits the extraction of information in terms of team member placement. All time spent with people in your network is productive time, because you're expanding your knowledge and your reputation. What you know about your people is currency. A solid team member is another stone in the pathway to achieving your goal.

## *Values matter*

### *Inspiration*

By knowing what inspires people, you can build consensus toward achieving the goal you're seeking to enlist their help with. As said above, knowing about the people whose allegiance you're building provides you with valuable information about their part in reaching the goal you have in mind. Maybe an ally is an unsung hero, laboring thanklessly in accounts. Maybe this ally has a strong understanding of an accounting methodology that can help move your project forward. Finding out what drives and inspires people to reach beyond where they currently are in life, or in your organization, is leverage to enlisting supporters and network participants. You all have something to give one another.

### *Recognition oriented factors*

Everyone likes to be recognized. But this is more important to some people than to others. Some folks fly just under the radar their entire lives, due to a lack of ambition, or being content with drawing a pay check and going home at the end of the day, unsung. Most of us aren't like that, though. We crave recognition for our contributions. It's helpful to be aware of this and it's also helpful to take note of those who aren't receiving the recognition they deserve for the work they're doing.

Bring these people into your circle and connect them with others like yourself who are goal-oriented and seeking competent support. This sets you apart as someone who recognizes the talent in other people. It also supports the project of moving toward the goal or goals you're striving to achieve. Strong talent on your team and on your side is the foundation of success. It also creates a network of appreciation for your recognition of that talent and that's powerful, as it supports your own recognition as a supportive, attentive and (most importantly) influential leader.

*Relationships matter*

Take the time to listen to people's problems, their life milestones and stories. Look at the baby pictures and be happy they're being shown to you, as this is a display of confidence and trust. Their lives matter and your interest in the details of their lives makes of you more than a co-worker or ally, it makes you a friend. People need to be heard. You don't have to offer them solutions to their problems, or even advice. All you have to do is listen. This is a skill every leader has – the ability to listen to people.

The listening ear is a powerful ear, invested with communal respect. The time you spend listening to others, even when the discussion is of a personal nature, is time which creates a bond which blurs the line between work and leisure. This is a value-added feature of business relationships which builds bridges between you and those you listen to. It builds workplace perceptions of your character, adding another dimension to it. Your likeability is a huge factor in your success and can't be underestimated. Likeability is a major part of influence, as people are much more likely to be on the side of someone they like and respect.

# Chapter 10: Your Influence Skill Set

## *Clarity of purpose*

An important facet of the ability to influence others is your own clarity. Know what you want and have a clear plan of how you're going to get it. Whether you're working in sales and trying to improve the team's quarterly figures, or trying to encourage a student to be more diligent with study, or to set them on a career path – know what the objective is, clearly. The only way you can succeed in influencing someone to behave in a desired way, is if you are clear about what you hope to achieve. You don't get in your car to drive to a destination you've never been without setting the GPS. The same goes for the application of influence toward achieving a desired effect or goal. Know where you're going.

Always be prepared in advance, with the following:

- A list of prioritized objectives.


- A clear picture of the final destination (what it looks like).


## *Preparing the environment*


If you are seeking to reach agreement with someone, you need to make them feel comfortable. You also need to be relaxed, yourself. At the same time, for effective communication (which is important when you want to influence someone's behavior, as this book is explaining) you need to make the environment conducive to your interaction. And you need to have in place a planned sequence of events at that meeting beforehand.


The best way to achieve this is to draw up a meeting agenda and circulate it to those who will attend, one day prior to the meeting. In this way, everyone knows what to expect and what shape the meeting will take. The agenda should make clear what the goals of the meeting are. Checking off the items on it should move you closer to agreement, if not enable all present to reach consensus to move forward. The logical sequence of events represented by following an agenda is a function of a critically structured plan. Having a plan of such quality never fails to impress.

## Consensus building

In building consensus, you're making it clear you are open to suggestion (which you should always be, regardless of your single minded focus on your ultimate goal). Building consensus employs those listening skills we talked about earlier. Hearing what people say and truly listening means you're not planning a response while they're talking. It means you're actively hearing everything they say. Subtext, word choice and tone are all important and so are your skills at hearing what's really being said. Proceeding with these skills in play can provide you with the basis for genuine and not false consensus.

False consensus is reached when people are "heard out", but not "heard". These are two entirely different animals. The first is condescending indulgence of hearing what no longer matters, because a decision has already been made and the results of that decision, imposed. Being heard means that influence on the final decision is still a possibility and that what's offered may result in concessions, if it features actual merit.

Being present to the input of others and being able to integrate their thoughts and suggestions into an existing plan is a function of leadership. Leadership is not imposed. Leadership is extended to others as a service. Consensus building is a way to bring forward the knowledge of the team and add it to your own. In the case of reaching agreement, it's the foundation of lasting relationships that won't later be ruptured by objections to not being heard. This is extremely important. Autocratic leadership is unwelcome and will not survive for long. It is a corrosive leadership style that is not sustainable.

## *Creating rapport*

When someone begins to enjoy your company, it becomes much easier for you to enlist their support. This makes it more likely they'll support your viewpoint in situations in which that counts. Allies are people who like and trust you. Your relationships are what will move your goals forward and create a foundation for your success and that of your allies, also. People, while perhaps not being entirely aware of this on an intellectual level, know this instinctively. That is why it is important that you prioritize establishing rapport with others. It's the basis of strong allegiances.

Part of creating rapport is establishing the common interests you hold with others. Taking an interest in them and offering them information about who you are is how this is achieved. Being too veiled about yourself makes you appear cold, calculating and detached. Establish that you're open and also, a person who can be trusted.

It's also important to establish ease with others and one way this can done is to mirror body language. You'll probably find (if you pay attention), that you do this anyway, when you've begun to establish rapport with someone. Mirroring body language sends the unconscious signal that there is a bond already established between two people and that they're on the same team. Mirroring speech patterns is another way of doing this. Repeating key words with enthusiasm at opportune times is another natural way we tell each other we're enjoying a conversation, or agreeing with each other. Nod, smile and respond positively when you sense a common theme emerging in conversation. This sends the message that you're accessible on the most basic, human level.

## Suggestions instead of demands

People routinely bridle at directives. In Western societies where individualism is a way of life, we like to believe in our personal autonomy as a value. That means it's not the best course of action to demand things from people. Much more effective is suggesting a course of action and building consensus based on the suggestion, while being open to input and concessions to other points of view. This is the democratic way of achieving goals and one that is completely manageable with the application of a deft hand.

Here are examples of language that gives your listener the option to chip in and yet still leaves you the "wiggle room" to get to where you believe you need to go:

- Would you be interested in doing a-b-c?


- Could you be interested in doing a-b-c?

- I think we should do a-b-c. What do you think?

- Do you think this is the best way forward, or do you have others ideas?

Leaving space for opinion and input, while still advancing the validity of your own opinion is the stuff of which influence is made. While you're providing people with a rationale for your point of view, your willingness to entertain amendments to that point of view only increases your influential power. Imposition rarely ends in anything but resentment. By building consensus through input and exchange, you will still arrive at the goal you have in mind, but you'll do it with the support of a willing team, signed on to the plan in question. A fringe benefit? That input will undoubtedly improve on the original plan and will result in satisfaction on the part of all involved.

### *Heightening your awareness*

Awareness of the responses of other people to what you're saying is a key to influential action. What are their facial expressions telling you? Their body language and their word choices? What about tone and pitch? All these factors are rich with information that you can draw on to temper your pitch and to get people on your side. It can also cue you to back off and change lanes, while you re-group and allow others their input.

Active listening, while employing body language (head nodding, eye contact) and assenting noises ("uh-huh", "yes", "I see") is also about deeply engaging with what's being said and the complementary messages being sent by the speaker. Your awareness in crucial situations, of all the factors that create a communicative environment, is of the utmost important. You need to be aware, not only of what's being said, but implications about what's intended, what's not being said and the speaker's frame of mind. All these factors work together to form a more concise body of information from which you may draw in order to apply influential action.

## *Matching the other person's communication style (mirroring)*

While outright mimicry is obviously out of the question, you can certainly seek to mirror the communication styles of the people you're engaging with, in order to help you establish rapport and common ground. Suppose someone looks at you for just a couple of seconds before looking down, or past you, and then looks back at you. This non-verbal style tells you something important about the person you're engaging – sustained eye contact is undesirable. So mirror that, in order to establish a comfortable level of communication that's implicitly agreed upon by both parties. This is an unspoken level of communication. By mirroring the tendencies of the other party, you are sending a message of respect and concession to the communication style being modelled.

## *Summing up your agenda*

At the conclusion of a business interaction, especially a meeting, it's important that you provide a summation of what you came into that meeting intending to do. In the course of your summation, you can acknowledge the importance of the feedback and input the exchange or meeting has provided. Pointing out that the feedback received was pivotal to the development of your agenda and enriched it, gets people on your bus and ready to roll. When people feel their opinions are valued, they will come along for the ride. They will also form part of a team that is more cohesive than if you hadn't included and then acknowledged the role their input played in reinforcing your foundational agenda.

The addition of the input of others to your narrative is a key component of consensus building as a part of influential action. It's a form of leadership outreach that not only strengthens the leader's position, but strengthens the agenda's integrity. Adding useful feedback and input can only build a better mousetrap. Good and successful leaders are keenly aware of this.

# Chapter 11: Scientifically Proven Methods of Non-Verbal Influence

We've discussed the need to read other people's attitudes and perspectives by observing their body language, as part of your influential arsenal. In any case, communication is a two-way interaction. You're also being "read" by those you interact with. Even if people don't boast the same level of awareness of non-verbal communication you do, they are still registering what you're saying without words. This is why it's so important that you master this aspect of communication in order to use it effectively. The perceptions of others are being shaped in every move you make, quite literally. This is true, even if that perception is subconscious. That subconscious impression can impact the willingness of others to work with and cooperate with you, so learning to send the right message is crucial.

Let's take a look at some aspects of body language and what they say to others, taking note of any habits you may model which need remediation:

## Dilated Pupils

As Psychologist Eckhard Hess established in 1975, your pupils dilate when you are highly interested in what the person talking is saying. When you notice the dilation of someone's pupils, you're in a good position to move further toward your goal of influencing that person to take your part in whatever goal it is you have in mind. Strike while the iron is hot. This applies to all spheres of your life - social, business life and family.

## Body Position

Being aware of how you're positioned in relation to those you're addressing is a fundamental skill. Are you facing them directly? Then it's important that other aspects of your body language don't indicate aggression, as facing someone directly can have that effect, if your hands are on your hips, your head is thrown back with your chin up, or you're standing too close to the other person. Placing your hands in front of you, with your fingers laced, is a non-confrontational way of saying you're not a threatening person. Placing your hands behind your back is another way, but may also be interpreted as submission, particularly if your feet are close together. With feet wider apart, this arm and hand position is much more effective and signals openness.

Turning away from someone may indicate that you're attempting to avoid a confrontation, or that you're not truly engaged in the conversation. In can also mean you don't trust or like the person in question. Again, the position of the arms and hands is key to understanding the message. Folding one arm across your chest to hold the arm closest the other party (as though half-hugging yourself), indicates shyness, as does wrapping both arms around the body in a self-hugging motion.

## Following your gaze

Someone who follows your gaze wherever you divert it, is likely to be a progressive thinker. Conservative thinkers will not do this. The gaze will remain fixed and static. Following the gaze is also an indication of mirroring, practiced either consciously or unconsciously. As we've discussed elsewhere, mirroring is a sign of familiarity and common cause, which generally means that we're reaching out to the other party without words.

## Physical/Verbal Dissonance

The person you are speaking to may present a calm and unruffled façade (or at least be endeavoring to do that. You may, at first glance, believe this person to be attentive to what you're saying, but there are signs that break through the façade. Being attentive to these can be helpful in determining whether the person you're talking to is either zoning out or is preoccupied.

Crossing and uncrossing the legs, when seated, is one such indication. Restless hands are another, including constant movement of the hands, adjusting clothing, picking at the fingernails, rubbing the fingers and lacing and unlacing the fingers. People who are not engaging with you, but who prefer to pretend that this is the case, instead of indicating an interest in ending the conversation, are either being unduly polite, or deliberately deceptive. The eyes can determine which of these is true.

Continual blinking is a strong signal that the person you're talking to is unwilling to continue the conversation, but even more unwilling to own up to their discomfort, boredom or need to move on to something else, as the time they've allotted to the discussion has elapsed.

### Stand with shoulders square

If you want the trust and support of others, you need to display resolute confidence. Maintaining a confident bearing involves good posture and squaring the shoulders while in conversation. When accompanied by similarly squaring your feet, this may seem confrontational, but can be very useful in establishing primacy in difficult situations. Body language like this is reasonably aggressive, but can be modified by placing the hands behind the back, or amplified by placing the hands on the hips (ultra-aggressive, as discussed earlier.

Of primary importance is good posture, which sends a strong

message of confidence and self-awareness.

## *Leaning in*

If you lean towards the person you're engaging, chances are that person is going to stop speaking and listen to what you have to say. This works, whether you are standing or seated. This posture tends to make you appear dominant. The other person will read leaning in to mean that you are serious about what you are saying and that you expect to be heard.

As you can see, your body language can influence other people by more intensely focusing your message; complementing your words with supportive physical cues. Being attentive to maintaining body language which correlates with your spoken message will not only make you more effective in your interactions with others, but signals your personal integrity. That's powerful.

# Chapter 12: The Social Psychology of Making Friends

Is it always easy to make friends in a new environment? Of course not! Sometimes it is extremely intimidating and at other times, downright hostile. Other times, you feel like fish out of water. Everybody needs friends and learning how to attract them is an important life skill we should all have. Human beings are fundamentally social animals who seek out the company of others and there are very few exceptions to that rule.

## *Choosing friends – Drawing the kind of friends you'd like to have*

Here are three broad categories of friends:

*Hello-Bye-bye friends (acquaintances)*

These are people who become your friends almost automatically, by virtue of finding yourselves in the same environment, like your workplace, for example. You say "hello" when you meet the first time in the day and you say "bye-bye" as you wind up for the day. Once away from the shared environment, these friends (which are actually only acquaintances) rarely have any further involvement with you. They're nice to know and they can be valuable allies, due to their skills, but they're not necessarily the sort of people you can count on one hand. (The Greeks say that you can count true friends on one hand – that's something to keep in mind).

*The Average Buddy*

Drinking buddies, golf buddies, shopping pals – fun time friends come and go. They share with you the things about life that make it fun, because they're fun. They like to laugh and enjoy your company. The lighter side of life is where these friends are going to pop up. These aren't necessarily people you engage in long conversations about the meaning of life, or the reality of climate change. This is your loose social circle, developed over time, that enjoys a good time as much as you do. They come and go and when you meet, a good time is had by all, but there's little in the way of depth in the relationship.

*Soul friends*

These are the 3:00 am phone call friends. You know

they'll be ready to talk if you wake them from a sound sleep. These are the people you can go on a road trip with and not want to kill before you've even hit Route 66.

Long, probing conversations, shared secrets and mutual support are what these friends are all about. People who stick with you, through thick and thin, are soul friends. They're the people who have an intimate understanding of what makes you tick and you return the favor. Some of these friends may be with you from childhood until death. Others, you may pick up along the way. What distinguishes them from the hello bye-byes and average buddies is the depth of the relationship. You may go years without seeing a soul friend, but when you finally meet up again, it's as though no time has passed. You pick up where you left off, because you know each other so well and you were meant to be friends. These are the ones who are the hardest to find and also the ones you long for. Soul friends are a reflection of who we are and what we really care about. Even more than that, they're the people we know we can always count on, because they know exactly who we are.

### *Forming genuine friendships takes time*

True friends are not made overnight. True, lasting and intimate friendships evolve over time, due to a genuine chemistry that exists between the people involved. Like romantic relationships, friendships are based in a fundamental chemical exchange which speaks to both parties like a song. You know when it's real. You can't create these bonds. They're pre-existing realities that you can only recognize and act on. When true friends; soul friends come into your life, the impact will be unforgettable. You will know immediately that the person you've just met is intended to be with you (in whatever capacity) until the end of your life. Soul friends may not always be at our side, physically, but they will always be at our side, spiritually. Where ever we are and whatever we're doing, we know they're there. We know we can pick up the phone, call and find them ready to talk to us. These are the friends who are with us until we're no longer living and breathing. That's what makes them so special and so incredibly important.

While we may recognize a soul friend at first sight, the world is not a place in which bonds are easily formed on this level. Soul friends, despite the distrust we've all learned to live with in the modern world, will look beyond that initial reticence and continue showing up. They won't give up. They'll seek you out, even when they don't know they're doing it and you'll do the same. Over time, the bond will become unbreakable and you will have made a friend for life.

Here is how you can become adept at making new friends:

*Don't over think*

Have you been apprehensive about meeting someone only for you to feel at home with them in the first two minutes of meeting? The fact is that if you are meeting a person for the first time, you have no idea how they are or how they behave.

Why bother analyzing everything half to death?

And again, assuming that meeting with a new person is bound to be scary only serves to make you fearful of the moment. The fear then makes you wary of the meeting; sometimes even making you detest it. In fact, for the most part, the reason you find yourself feeling somewhat shy towards a person is because of the fear you are harboring of having an encounter with them, or anyone else for that matter. Life makes us into individual silos of isolation. It makes us suspicious. Bad experiences with other people can stunt our ability to form the kind of bonds we're actually hungry for – the kind of bonds that last a life time. The best solution, therefore, is to disabuse yourself of the notion that meeting people you are not familiar with is scary. Stop over-thinking about how to carry out that first conversation; how to connect with people who are actually the kind of people you need in your life. Overthinking the forging of the most important connections in our lives can make of us sad, isolated people who never really connect with others in the profound and lasting way that human beings were intended to connect.

After all, who is to tell if the other party is not anxious about meeting you? We're all anxious in these latter days. We're all suspicious and nervous and continually asking ourselves if the people we meet have the right motivations; if they're genuine. Most of us are thinking the same thing. We've lost our trust in one another.

So relax and create in your mind a positive image of that first encounter; a healthy image. In any case, there are plenty of people out there who may judge you unfairly on your first encounter. Everyone carries around a collection of cultural assumptions about the composition of people who are worth knowing. You have them too. The trick is to open yourself to others and to allow the universe to connect you. It works very well, if you'll allow it to happen. People worth having as friends know better than to judge a person on superficial grounds. In summary, fear is in your mind – get rid of it! Let go of your accumulated fears and presuppositions and, instead, rely on your intuitive powers and your newly-established ability to read people. You know enough to understand when people are honest or not. You've learned to read their mannerisms, their speech patterns, their facial expressions and other non-verbal indicators about who they are. Trust yourself and your knowledge. You're more than ready to sift the wheat from the chaff, which means there's absolutely nothing to fear; no cause for suspicion or reticence.

You're now more than ready to throw yourself out into the social whirl and find the kind of people who deserve to have as friends. With your new skills, rooted in the practice of social psychology, you're going to be able to establish rather quickly who is naughty and who is nice. The Big Bad Wolf is out there, but you're not Little Red Riding Hood anymore. You're now a proficient and capable, socially aware person. No one's pulling the wool over your eyes anymore. With your new knowledge, it will be easy for you to discern, from the people you meet, who is going to be the kind of friend you need in your life. There's no more guesswork, because you know the ropes now.

*Move at your own pace*

If you have been out of the social scene for a while, you may feel overwhelmed meeting new people, as you ease yourself back into it (say in a seminar or even a party). However, you can pre-empt that problem by seeking out individual friends or acquaintances who you expect to be in attendance. You can meet with them before the event and catch up. This will put you more at ease with throwing yourself back into the social whirl. By the time you get to the event you won't feel as anxious. For one, you'll know people who are going to be there. They can introduce you to other people. For another, your friends will be aware that you're anxious. They'll shepherd you. Never be shy about reaching out to people you know for support. As we've learned in the course of this book – that's what friends are for.

Just in case you are you're seeking to move back into having a social life again, after having been a little sequestered, here are some great ways to ease yourself back in:

- Begin by reaching out to acquaintances – the hello-bye bye category is a good place to start. There's not a lot to lose here.

- Extend your social circle to include small groups of people you are friends with, just to observe the dynamics of people relating; familiarizing yourself with being around groups of people again. It doesn't have to be scary. You can ease yourself back in.

- Expand your social circle by accompanying your friends when they are meeting with others. Make it known that you're hoping to move back into a more active social life. Most people will be happy to help you do that.

- Break out of your comfort zone and begin accepting invitations to mix with people, even those not in your close circle of friends. They say that you can't get to the sweetest fruit without going out on a limb, so climb out there. Learn to relish the opportunity to have new experiences with new people. You're learning more about yourself now and about other people. Why not get out there and put some of that knowledge into practice? After all, why shouldn't people want to meet someone as interesting and intelligent as you are?

*Be pro-active in socializing*

Once you you've become re-acquainted with the practice of seeking out new social connections and when you are no longer in your solitary cocoon, you can begin to pro-actively seek out people you know and others who are new to you. You can begin branching out from the foundation that your friends and acquaintances have provided by moving further into the social milieu, into areas that may be a little unfamiliar. For example:

- Join a group or groups whose members share your hobbies and other interests.

- Enroll to participate in workshops or to pursue courses of study which interest you. It's quite easy to make friends in a group in which all the members share a common interest.

- Volunteer and you'll be happy to serve as you make new friends in the process. While you're at it, you'll develop skills and aptitudes you may have hoped to make more viable. In the same way as workshops or groups, the common core of interest will provide a jumping off point for bonding with others volunteering with you.

- Accept invitations to birthday parties, various celebrations, and other social functions. You never know who'll meet at gatherings like these. Break through you own barriers. These may be preventing the type of people you want to connect with from connecting with you.

- Be open to attending social events and even "meet ups", based on common interests. It also doesn't hurt to go out to the bar every now and again. There are people sitting in bars in every city of the world, just looking for someone interesting to talk to. Maybe, just like you, they're looking for a way out of isolation, or social stagnation. Your horizons expand when you demand that they do. No one is going to push them outward for you.

- Join online communities – while these may be located in cyberspace, but I know personally that they can result in real world friendships. I've made many real world friends on Facebook and other online communities. Sometimes, it's easier to share your thoughts in writing, than it is in spoken conversation. This is just one more avenue for making the kind of lasting connections you're hoping to. BONUS: You get to analyze the written communication style of potential new friends before you actually meet them!

*Take the initiative*

There's no reason you should wait for others to approach you. They're just as reserved as you are, after all. Nobody is born knowing anyone else unless they're family and even then, it's a bit of a crapshoot. You can approach people to start a conversation, by employing simple questions, like "how are you" and "where are you from". It's not hard and you've absolutely nothing to lose. Be open to the people around you and you'll be surprised at how readily they'll respond to that openness.

Remember you are trying to break the ice between you and a stranger, so avoid over-talking. Be warm, but not overly insistent and don't get discouraged if others don't respond immediately. Always try to put yourself in the place of the other person. Employ the lessons you've learned in this book to figure out where they stand and try to meet them there. Be gentle in your judgments of others, though, remembering always that we all judge one another. Take the time to let the person you're engaging revealing themselves to you, just as they're hoping you'll reveal yourself to them.

*Fight any temptation to be judgmental*

No one's perfect and that includes you. We tend to evaluate people quite harshly before we get to know them. This is a function of our survival instinct, which tells us that the fewer people we allow near us, the less potential there is for danger. But we're modern people and we can do better than that. Besides, you now have in your command a variety of skills concerning non-verbal language that can help you sift through the people who very obviously aren't the sort of folks you're looking for.

Remaining open to those we meet is the door to better friendships and more of them. Not writing people off because of petty complaints about the way they look, or speak, or dress is the best way we can become more flexible about who we welcome as friends and that's the real secret. Sometimes, it's the most unlikely person who is going to prove to be our very best and long-term friend. Everyone is looking for the kind of friends we believe we deserve, but we should always ask ourselves if we meet our own qualifications. You may find that, in asking yourself this question honestly, you discover shortcomings in yourself you might not be willing to tolerate in other people. As I've said repeatedly in this book, knowing yourself is the key to knowing other people, so don't overlook amending your own challenges before you start writing other people off as potential friends, due to their own.

# Conclusion

People are not as mysterious as they seem and understanding them is not so much a science, as an observational project. Your powers of observation, when it comes to navigating situations at home, with friends and at work, are well within your ability to understand and command. It's all a matter of picking up the clues people liberally offer, as we engage with them.

Now that you understand how Social Psychology applies to your every day life and how you can use it to improve your business, your career and even your social life, you can start implementing the skills you've learned. You'll be surprised at how fast you'll see positive changes. You'll begin to experience better rapport between you and your co-workers and family, as well as your friends. You'll be more readily able to understand where people are coming from and be less inclined to walk out of any number of incidents and experiences frustrated, asking yourself "What are they thinking?" You now have the tools to accurately read people's emotional and intellectual responses more accurately and that makes you a much more effective and professional person.

This book is a popularization of the amalgam resulting from the melding of sociology and psychology – social psychology. While the two disciplines may still be at odds with one another, when they're reconciled they form a system for interpreting the world around us in very effective and constructive ways. By paying close attention to other people, you'll be able to more confidently move through life. The foundation of that ability is knowing yourself and being in command of the way you present yourself to others. By curating your public presence, you'll be more readily able to discern the undercurrents of other people's psychological and emotional landscapes and to glean important information that will help you live a more successful and peaceful life.

Human beings are complex animals and you're no exception. Knowing your tics and mannerisms is the roadmap to understanding those of others and your ticket to being able to successfully influence them for the good. As I've tried to make clear throughout this book, my goal is to make other people more easily interpretable to you. By detailing some of the primary ways people communicate non-verbally, I hope I've been able to show you how people are much less mysterious than they seem at first glance. Life is a mystery, but people aren't really. People are open books, offering you a wealth of information in the way they present themselves to you. The way they hold themselves, speak, arrange their faces and move their hands. This is all free information which can help you become much more successful at getting a handle on your interactions with others.

You're now able to use the information in this book to be better at everything you do. Every day is a new beginning and every person you meet represents a multitude of possibilities. Every single encounter is a link in the chain of your life. With the knowledge in this book, I'm hoping you'll come to understand how great an opportunity every connection you make is. Everyone you meet, from the bus driver to the CEO of your company, to the spin class instructor, to the barista at your local coffee bar, is an important link in the chain of your life. There's no one person who's going to make a difference to you (although, they're out there and they can be part of it). Your life is a series of encounters that lead to your goals and dreams and each of those encounters is as rich as you make it.


I hope the knowledge you've gained by reading this will lead you forward, and that your journey will be peopled with the kind of intelligent and lively folks that will make it a thrilling tapestry of experience. Sometimes the destination is fun to think about, but if we miss the journey on the way there, we miss out on the best part. Look up from the path, see who's walking with you and then ask yourself – what did they mean by that hand movement? What does that facial expression mean? How do my own mannerisms mirror theirs? You'll figure out what it all means while you're on your way. Just don't forget to enjoy the journey. It really is the very best part.

65609990R00060

Made in the USA
Middletown, DE
01 March 2018